SLEEPING IN SPACE

Tracie Santos

Rourke
Educational Media

A Division of
Carson
Dellosa
Education

Before Reading: *Building Background Knowledge and Vocabulary*

Building background knowledge can help children process new information and build upon what they already know. Before reading a book, it is important to tap into what children already know about the topic. This will help them develop their vocabulary and increase their reading comprehension.

Questions and Activities to Build Background Knowledge:

1. Look at the front cover of the book and read the title. What do you think this book will be about?
2. What do you already know about this topic?
3. Take a book walk and skim the pages. Look at the table of contents, photographs, captions, and bold words. Did these text features give you any information or predictions about what you will read in this book?

Vocabulary: *Vocabulary Is Key to Reading Comprehension*

Use the following directions to prompt a conversation about each word.

- Read the vocabulary words.
- What comes to mind when you see each word?
- What do you think each word means?

Vocabulary Words:
- cosmonaut
- g-force
- modules
- orbit
- purification
- resistant

During Reading: *Reading for Meaning and Understanding*

To achieve deep comprehension of a book, children are encouraged to use close reading strategies. During reading, it is important to have children stop and make connections. These connections result in deeper analysis and understanding of a book.

Close Reading a Text

During reading, have children stop and talk about the following:

- Any confusing parts
- Any unknown words
- Text-to-text, text-to-self, text-to-world connections
- The main idea in each chapter or heading

Encourage children to use context clues to determine the meaning of any unknown words. These strategies will help children learn to analyze the text more thoroughly as they read.

When you are finished reading this book, turn to the next-to-last page for **After-Reading Questions** and an **Activity**.

TABLE OF CONTENTS

TO THE STARS

In 1961, Yuri Gagarin, a **cosmonaut**, was the first human to journey into outer space. He stayed in space for 108 minutes before returning to Earth. Ever since then, astronauts have continued to make their dreams about space a reality. Scientists and engineers have worked hard to get them there.

cosmonaut (KOS-mo-nawt): an astronaut in a Russian or Soviet Union space program; in Greek, *kosmo* means "universe" and *nautes* means "sailor"

Yuri Gagarin traveled around Earth once and reached a height of 203 miles (327 kilometers).

Command **modules** and space shuttles were used by the National Aeronautics and Space Administration (NASA) to send humans to space. But after 2011, NASA has relied on countries such as Russia to get there. Now, astronauts have even more opportunities to explore space as privately-owned space travel companies prepare for liftoff.

modules (MAH-jools): pieces of a spacecraft that can be separated and used by themselves, usually for a specific purpose

A Partnership in Space

In 2020, SpaceX, a privately-owned company, launched a rocket carrying four astronauts and supplies into space. The rocket was named the Falcon 9 after the famous *Star Wars* ship, the Millennium Falcon. It is also reusable! It has been launched 102 times so far.

Above us, astronauts **orbit** Earth inside the *International Space Station (ISS)*. People have used this spacecraft since the year 2000! For over 20 years, astronauts from many different countries have lived together and shared the modules that make up the *ISS.* In that time, they've discovered the many ways that living in space is different from living on Earth. They have also found ways to make living in space easier.

orbit (OR-bit): a path described by one object revolving around another

Sleeping in the Stars

Since the 1960s, astronauts from many countries have stayed in space for long-term missions. The longest singular mission was completed by Russian cosmonaut Valeri Polyakov, who was there for 437 days. Astronauts Jerry Ross and Franklin Chang-Diaz are tied for the record of most trips to space—an amazing seven launches!

SOLVING SPACE PROBLEMS

In the 8 minutes and 42 seconds that it takes to launch into space, astronauts experience **g-force**. Some astronauts describe it as a crushing feeling that makes it hard to breathe.

Scientists wanted to fix this. By 1966, they invented a material that evenly distributed body weight and pressure to make passengers more comfortable. You may have heard of it! This material is called memory foam. It is so comfortable that people now use it for mattresses.

g-force (jee-fors): the force of gravity or acceleration on a body

People make messes, even astronauts. However, messes can be very dangerous inside a spacecraft. Water and other materials can damage or break the computers. They can also clog the systems that bring breathable air into a spacecraft.

The Russian space station Mir was in use for 12 years before it experienced these technical issues. When astronauts opened up a panel for inspection, they found football-sized water pockets floating inside! The *ISS* uses a different filter system and tools such as cordless vacuums to keep the space station sparkling.

Mir is no longer in space. In 2001, Russian space officials removed it from orbit with a controlled fall into the Pacific Ocean.

You can't just turn on a faucet in space! So, where do astronauts get water to drink and bathe? They recycle it! Water **purification** is another advancement that scientists have made in space travel.

The *ISS* recycles sweat, water molecules from breathing, and even urine into reusable water. The process takes out any contamination, so the water is safe to use.

purification (PYOOR-uh-fi-KAY-shun): the process of making something pure or clean

Can You Shower in Space?

Every drop of water is important in space. Astronauts on the *ISS* bathe with liquid soap and no-rinse shampoo. This uses much less water than taking a shower on Earth would.

Fighting Earth's gravity keeps our bones and muscles strong. But on the *ISS*, there is almost no gravity. Astronauts must exercise for two hours every day to keep their bones and muscles healthy. That's why the *ISS* has a gym! The treadmill uses bungee cords and a harness to keep the astronauts in place. It also has a weightlifting machine that uses vacuum tubes. Using it feels like using real weights on Earth.

All Work, No Play? No Way!

Even astronauts need time to relax. Some talk to people on Earth via phone or email and listen to music. Some create music! Canadian astronaut Chris Hadfield was aboard the *ISS* in 2013. He used his free time to record a cover of David Bowie's "Space Oddity" with his guitar. The video has over 40 million views.

Just like on Earth, astronauts need somewhere to sleep after a long day. You might have a mattress with pillows and a comfortable blanket at home. In space, astronauts sleep in sleeping bags. They are clipped or strapped down so that they do not float around while they sleep. And because space has no "up" or "down," they can sleep in any direction.

Healthy sleep also means a healthy sleep pattern. If your sleep pattern is interrupted, it can change your mood and make it hard to move and think. On Earth, people can tell when it is time to sleep and wake up because of when the sun rises and sets. But astronauts experience a sunrise or sunset every 90 minutes! How do they make sure they are sleeping well?

Astronauts can use medicine and special blue lights to help them sleep. Another solution is to make spacecraft very comfortable for astronauts so they can relax. Scientists are still trying to solve the problem of how to sleep in space.

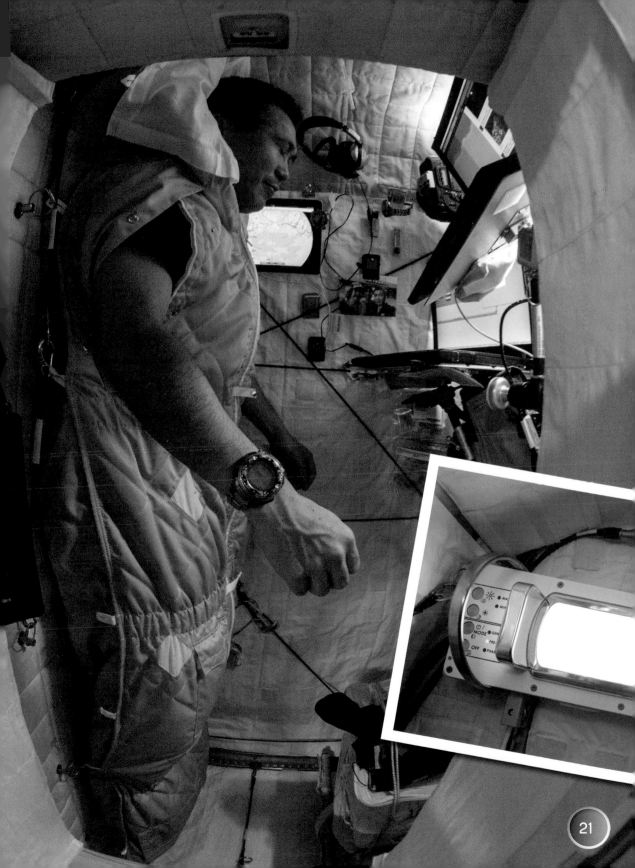

A JOB IN SPACE

It's not all fun and games aboard the *ISS*. These astronauts are on missions, and they have work to do. A workday in space is 12 hours long! Astronauts need to conduct experiments and collect information. Since the *ISS* has been in use, astronauts have researched how to grow food in space and the long-term effects of living without Earth's gravity. They have also studied Earth's own environment and even how to treat medical conditions in space.

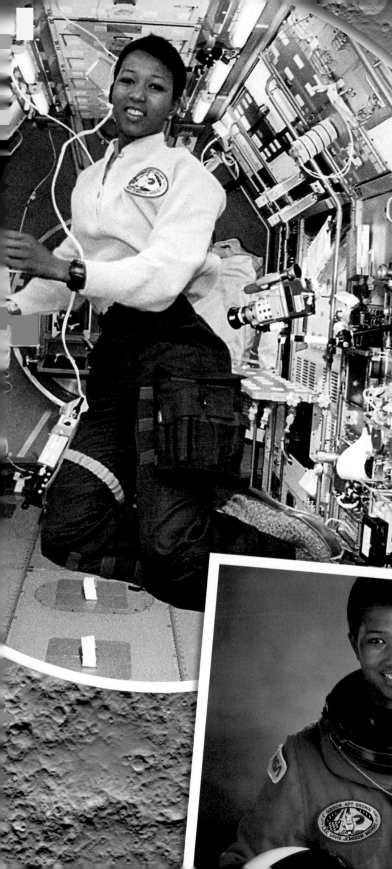

Dr. Who?

Dr. Mae Jemison, that's who! Jemison was the first African American woman in space. Remember the reason that astronauts have to exercise so much? Jemison was one of the lead investigators on experiments that studied the effects of space flight on bone cells. The goal was to understand why they become weaker.

Not all work can be done from inside a spacecraft. Repairs and some research have to be done in space. But space can be very dangerous. How do astronauts get their jobs done? Robots can sometimes help. Long robot "arms" can reach out to pick up rocks, dust samples, and more, so astronauts do not have to go outside the spacecraft.

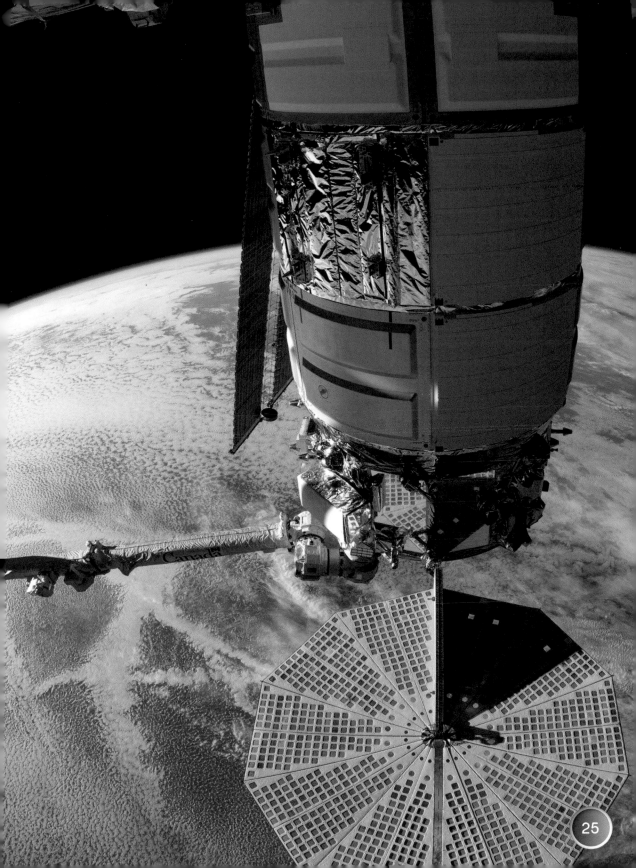

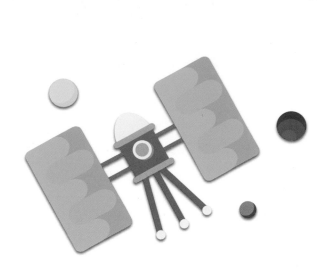

When robot arms can't get the job done, an astronaut might need to put on their space suit and do it themselves. A lot of work has gone into making space suits safe and comfortable. They are **resistant** to the extreme cold and heat of space. They also have a special system that provides oxygen to astronauts.

resistant (ri-ZIS-tuhnt): able to withstand or fight off something

On the Move

Space suits alone can weigh over 280 pounds (127 kilograms). They also make it more difficult to move. Astronauts must be physically fit so they can move around and still do their jobs.

S. RYZHIKOV

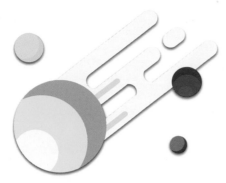

Life in space is very different than life on Earth. Many incredible things have been invented to make space travel and work safer and more comfortable. That happened because people used their imaginations to solve problems. What space solutions can you think of? You might be the person who makes the next great space invention.

The International Space Station Diagram

As of February 2021, three spaceships are docked at the *ISS*: the SpaceX Crew Dragon, Russia's Progress 75, and the Soyuz MS-17.

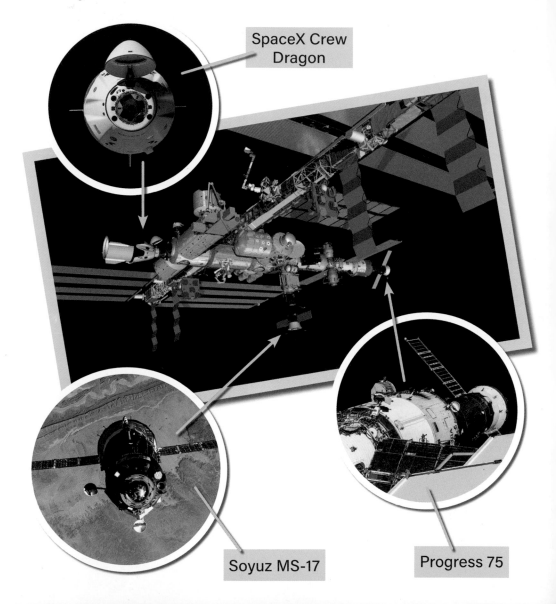

SpaceX Crew Dragon

Soyuz MS-17

Progress 75

Index

After-Reading Questions

1. How do astronauts bathe?

2. What material is used to make g-force more comfortable?

3. Look at the *ISS* diagram on page 30. How do you think the spacecraft gets its electricity?

4. Who was the first African American woman in space?

5. Why do messes need to be cleaned up quickly in space?

Activity

Think about a daily activity in your life that might be difficult in space. Write down the things that would make it difficult. Design a solution to make that activity safer, easier, or both during space travel. Make a model of your invention using items from around your home.

About the Author

As a child, Tracie Santos loved learning about the mysteries of space. Today, she writes about science and the amazing things we find on Earth and beyond. She especially loves Laika, the hero dog who was the first animal to orbit Earth.

www.rourkeeducationalmedia.com

PHOTO CREDITS: cover: ©klagyivik/ Getty Images; cover: ©forplayday/ Getty Images; cover: ©LineTale/ Shutterstock.com; pages 4-5: ©mechanick/ Getty Images; pages 4-8, 10-16, 18, 20, 22-24, 26-28, 30-31: ©Helen Field/ Getty Images; page 5: ©NASA; pages 6-7: ©SPACEX/UPI/Newscom; page 7: ©Polaris/ Newscom; page 7: ©SPACEX/NASA; pages 8-9: ©Nasa/ZUMA Press/Newscom; pages 10-11: ©SPACEX/NASA; page 11: © Steve Thurow/U.S. Air Force/ CNP/Newscom; pages 12-13: ©Elena11/ Shutterstock.com; page 13: ©NASA; pages 14-15: ©Brian Dunbar/NASA; page 15: ©AiWire/Newscom; pages 16-17: ©ESA/Sipa USA/Newscom Special; pages 18-19: ©ESA/Sipa USA/Newscom; page19: ©Nasa/ZUMA Press/Newscom; pages 20-21: © Nasa; page 21: © Nasa; pages 22-23: ©Nasa/ZUMA Press/Newscom; page 23: ©Nasa/ZUMA Press/Newscom; pages 24-25: ©Nasa/ZUMA Press/Newscom; pages 26-27: ©NASA/UPI/ Newscom; page 27: ©Andrey Shelepin/Nasa/ZUMA Press/Newscom; pages 28-29: ©Nasa/UPI/Newscom; page 29: ©Nasa/ZUMA Press/Newscom; page 30: ©Nasa/UPI/Newscom; page 30: ©Mark Garcia/Nasa Blogs; page 30: ©Nasa/ZUMA Press/Newscom; page 30: ©Nasa/ZUMA Press/Newscom

Edited by: Madison Capitano
Cover and interior design by: Alison Tracey

Library of Congress PCN Data

Sleeping in Space / Tracie Santos
(Reaching for the Stars)
ISBN 978-1-73164-892-1 (hard cover)(alk. paper)
ISBN 978-1-73164-840-2 (soft cover)
ISBN 978-1-73164-944-7 (e-Book)
ISBN 978-1-73164-996-6 (ePub)
Library of Congress Control Number: 2021935282

Rourke Educational Media
Printed in the United States of America
01-1662111937